Above the p line

by

Sarah Parsons-Winter

Above the Poverty line - Introduction

I really never expected to go to Africa. I hadn't travelled out of the UK until I was 25. I'd had holidays in this country aplenty and been to Europe, but Africa was in another league. I'd also heard stories of Africa, of violence and famine and hardship and tribal wars. I'd heard that your luggage goes missing and you get ripped off at every opportunity. I also knew it was incredibly hot and dusty - why would anyone want to go to Africa? Now I would ask you why don't you want to go to Africa? It would appear that God has done a work in me that has so changed my thinking and allowed me to give my heart to Africa and put Africa in my heart. Within a 2 year period the Lord took me to Africa eight times and I want to talk about my adventures and change your heart towards Africa too, maybe. I have specifically been to Kenya in the East of Africa, with part of the country touching the coast of the Indian Ocean.

I live in the UK and Kenya is part of the Commonwealth which means it is possible for me to get a visa for a year as a UK citizen, (It's just cheaper if you are going more than once to get the annual visa). but you can, with everyone else, buy your visa at the door when you arrive. (These rules have now changed and you may have to apply before you fly). It really doesn't make passport control any quicker, and if I did have a down side to Kenya, it would be passport control.

Waiting an hour to get through the passport control late at night is difficult and a lesson every time for me on grace. Those who control the department have a tendency of taking those from the back of a line and directing them to a nearly empty line, which means that effectively they have pushed in.

I now deliberately pick the longest line and give the rest up to God to see how long He will have me wait there!

The first time I went I got worried about my luggage, but it was there waiting for me when I finally came through to the airport to meet my contacts. I have in all my visits never lost or had anything stolen. I have had the occasion when I have paid more for something than it was worth, but most of the time I am aware of that. Sometimes I let it go and sometimes I don't. I am led by the Spirit and His heart of compassion is greater than mine - that is why I stay quiet. He knows much better than I do if someone has eaten that day, or even that week. I don't. Often in desperation people do things that are seen as ripping you off, but they have a family to feed and bills to pay and a home to try and hang on to. You may be thinking that it doesn't make it right to encourage corruption. I'm not talking about the government ripping off the money from the people into some off shore account. I'm talking about the taxi driver in his battered car charging you too much for a trip across town. I usually know when it's happening because I suddenly get cross. My discernment button has been activated and I know beyond a doubt that someone is trying it on. It's then that I go back to God for instructions.

Just to let you know that in the eight visits it has only happened a few times. I'm just saying that for those who think it's all corruption, to dispel some myths.

God connected me to my 'point' man in Kenya via Facebook. You could call Bishop Mickey my host, or Bishop, but he is the man God sent me to work with and every time I go it is different. The first time we communicated was when Mickey asked me to be his friend on Facebook.
I have lots of Godly people as friends on Facebook so was happy to add him on. What I didn't expect was the instant desire I would get in my Spirit to pray for Mickey and the fact that God would give me a message for him on our first encounter. We didn't connect for a couple of months after that and then he dropped by on Facebook to say hello again and the same thing happened again. God was up to something and I was curious about what He would do next. Well, you could have knocked me over with a feather, as they say here, I was surprised to be asked to write a message to Mickey's church for their 12th anniversary service.

He told me that the words I had given him had proven true and he wanted me to ask God for a word for his church. I was so honoured and told him that I would be delighted. I never did write a letter because when I asked God for something to write He told me that He was sending me there instead! I had wondered why I'd had a cheque in the post the day before, which turned out to be just what I would need to pay for the visa, injections and tablets that I would need for the trip.

I was beyond excited and a little scared too if I am honest. I was going to Africa alone. It was decided with prayer that I should stay with Mickey and his family, so they could look after me and I would be safe.

I can tell you how God provided for the trip - one person paid for the flight out, and another for the flight back, and a third came through with the expenses money. I hadn't asked for anything, just shared my vision, and God spoke to hearts and they offered to support what I was doing. So humbling and so encouraging too. So I ended up on an eight hour flight to Kenya with what the Lord had given me.

As we went over Kenya's airspace I had a major wobble and went to hide in the loo for a while, asking God all sorts of question and not all of them, well hardly any of them faith filled! What was I doing there? He was sending me to Africa with only one word, one six letter word to pass on to this Bishop and his church. What would they think!

Mickey and his family were so welcoming, and so gracious. They were there making sure I had things that were outside the norm for them. The majority of people in Kenya tend to eat with their fingers at home and I was given knife and fork, for which I was, and still am so grateful. I hadn't even thought about that! Also they heated water for me to wash with for the first few days when I arrived because there was no water in the building. How frustrating to have a shower but not to be able to use it because the water hadn't been pumped up. The same with the power, sometimes it works and sometimes it doesn't, and this is in Nairobi.

It wasn't like I was in some backwater, but the capital city. It's actually amazing how quickly I learnt to adapt and change my habits to accommodate these little hiccups. I was also told not to drink anything but bottled water because of the building work in Nairobi and the waste pipes leaking into the water supply! I commend the Kenyan people for just getting on with life even with these difficulties. What incredibly resilient people they are.

About seventy percent of worker's wages in Kenya goes on food, which is massive compared to about 20 - 30 percent for the UK. I knew I needed to pay my way and bless those I was staying with. I would learn from not only this visit, but all the ones that followed about the hospitality of the people in Kenya.
They had such a desire to have you stay in their home. I have had many people pray that I will stay. It is considered a blessing to receive visitors and that impacted me very much.

When I was there I also learnt that unemployment is 80 percent and there is little government help for those who have no jobs. With this being the case many try to earn a living selling goods on the street, it must be such a hard life. I heard of a Pastor who was trying to make a little money carrying 200 kg sacks for 200 shillings a time. The sack was so heavy that he could only manage one a day and the 200 shillings is about one pound fifty pence, hardly enough to feed his family of four.

Another delight to Kenyan life are the buses, they usually only travel when they are full, which is actually good for the environment, but not good if you have to sit and wait for an hour whilst it fills up. Imagine being at your local bus station and the driver just sits there until the bus is packed full, asking you to budge over so they can squeeze three people on to two seats, and then they bring out the wooden plank which is put across the gap so another one or two can also sit down. Those on the plank get charged the same rate as those on the seats, and if you are in an estate car they will try and squeeze in at least 12 people. four in the front, four in the back seat and four in the boot. All will be charged the same rate and if you don't like it you can buy more than one seat, or walk if you prefer. The worst seat is the one next to the driver where you have to elevate your leg so as not to knock the car out of gear whilst travelling. Try doing that for two hours and you will see why I didn't like that.

Over the years I tend to pay for a cab, it's more expensive but I don't get so cross at the greed of the bus drivers. I would rather have cheaper accommodation and pay a little more to get around. It works better for me.

With 70 percent of most money earned going on food it is understandable to see how everyone is affected by even the smallest price rises. I have this quote from Nelson Mandela on my study pin board and it really speaks to me. It says "Poverty is not an accident. Like slavery and apartheid, it is man-made and can be removed by the actions of human beings." It is so true and makes me question each time I read it, 'what do you want me to do God?'

Parents go without food so their children can learn, that makes me feel small to think about that one. I have seen parents reduce their portion sizes so their children can have more. I have seen parents say they are not hungry so others can eat. I know that happens here in the UK as well, but to see it first hand does something to my heart. These people are such heroes. They wouldn't say so. They would say they are just doing what they have to do to get by. I know that I have never been in that situation. Yes, I have gone without for my child, but not sacrificed my dinner for him. I have so much to thank God for.

There is the consensus of opinion that those parents in Africa should just have less children, and I believe that is what is happening. Many adults I have spoken to were one of eight or ten children, but they have only two or three children of their own. With medical help being provided the size of the family is getting smaller.

Now it's time to leave the stories behind of the things I have learnt about the culture and share my story, enjoy.

Above the Poverty line - Chapter One

I'd had an uneventful flight and landed at Nairobi airport.
It was about 9pm and I'd been up since 4.30am. Following
the signs through the airport was easy as they were all in
English and before I knew it I was in the passport visa line
to pay my fee (current fees on Kenyan Embassy Website)
for a single entry visa. It was hot in the line. It was
November 2011 and the Kenyan summer. I waited for
nearly an hour, the lines seemed to be moving really
slowly and when I got near the desk I started to be
concerned for my luggage. Would it still be there when I
got to it? I had heard stories of bags going missing, so each
time the thought came, I would pray. Then I would wonder
if the Bishop had come to meet me, again I would turn this
concern to prayer. Then I would ask myself what was I
doing here, on my own, across the other side of the world
in Africa? Then I would have to remember to breathe. I
was at times in the queue, close to tears. What was I
thinking? But I got to the desk, passed through without
any problems, collected my bags, also without problems.
Now to go to meet the Bishop and move in with him and
his family for 10 days, with people I had never met, in a
town I knew nothing about, in a continent that had so
many troubling stories.

I walked outside and the first thing I saw was a piece of paper with 'Sarah Parsons-Winter' written on it and then two smiling faces. I recognised the Bishop and his wife Rozah from the Facebook pictures – things were looking like they might be okay especially as I had my luggage too.

The Bishop, who I will call Mickey from now on, took us to a table and chairs of the closed café at the airport and there, in front of all the people, we joined hands and prayed, thanking God that I was there safely. The prayers we said openly, publicly and that was so refreshing. We got in a taxi and I was feasting my eyes on my first sights of Nairobi. It looked like the news footage on the BBC. So many people still in the streets. Evening sellers walking in the road trying to sell things to motorists. Who would be out trying to sell oranges and bananas at 10.30 pm on a Friday night unless you had to, unless you needed the money? I had just had my first introduction to poverty in Kenya.

We turned off the road and the taxi started going down dirt tracks with large potholes. There were still people around, stalls open, fires burning, music playing somewhere very loud with a heavy beat. Then we pulled up outside a block of flats – all breeze blocks and metal bars. We went up two flights of stairs in the pitch dark and every step was a different size. We had to take it slowly. Then I went into a flat, walking straight into the living room.

There was a three piece suite, a table, TV on a stand in the corner and through the hatch that leads to a kitchen is a new face – Esther, the house maid, or nannie, or both. I am taken to a bedroom with bunk beds and a mosquito net and it is explained that there is no running water at the moment. At that moment my heart sinks – how am I going to cope for 10 days. I am so used to things working. I even dislike camping because it's so primitive.

There is a bucket of water in the toilet and when it needs it, you pour the water down. The room next door is the shower room. I give out the gifts I have brought and head off to bed. I had thought long and hard about the sort of gifts I should bring, it's difficult with a different culture to know what to do. So I stuck with coffee, soap, and chocolates. I am told not to drink the water, only to use the bottled stuff. There is a lot of building work going on in Nairobi and the sewage and water pipes both get cracked and water mingles from both. I brush my teeth from a travel mug I've brought and I go to bed. You can hear the mosquitoes buzzing around the net, trying to get to you, but I know I'm safe underneath.

The next morning I offer up some shillings towards my keep. I can't expect those I have come to bless to cover my food expenses too. I was, after all, saving on hotel costs and eating out.

I realised much later on that I was in the room that Esther, the housemaid, would usually sleep in. She was bedded down, lying on cardboard and blankets on the floor in the kitchen. No persuasion would entice her to share the second bunk in the room I was using.

I was being honoured and treated as a special guest. Lovely, kind, thoughtful and also very humbling.

Next morning I woke up around 7am and ventured out of my room when I heard voices. There were three children of six and seven, two belonging to Mickey and Rozah and a niece staying for a while. They became very shy when they saw me. For many children, especially in the slum areas, they have never seen a white person.

With such diversity on the streets in the UK it seems incredible to think that could be the case, but they were fascinated to touch my arms, hold my hands and stroke my hair.

Back to getting ready in the flat I am offered a large bowl of hot water to wash with and accept it gratefully, so thankful that I thought to pack a tumbler at the last moment. Just what I need for washing my hair. I hadn't packed a dressing gown but just a shawl over my cotton PJ's.

I had white bread and margarine with tea for breakfast. I asked what time to be ready to go out and was ready by 9am, the time they told me. It surprised Mickey that the time he had said I had stuck to. Timing is different in Africa. The roads are bad, traffic jams can be long and if it rains, everything grinds to a standstill. Buses run when they are full so you have to wait for enough passengers. People are more laid back about waiting. It's not considered as rude to keep someone waiting like it is in the UK.

So, Saturday and we are heading off to the church at Jerico. I have brought a pink rucksack to transport my things around with me and Mickey insists on carrying it for me. It is safer that way, he doesn't seem to mind the colour. It's the special celebration for the church, 12 years, and they are making a weekend of it. Three things are happening in the tents on the field. In one free eye tests, in another free legal advice and the one I am in has prayer. I am asked to help pray. Compare that to a western celebration with cake, face painting and a bouncy castle! Mickey lets me take the lead.

I know he is testing me, seeing how I will handle the situations, but also he is acting as interpreter.

I am glad of his help — The first guy that came for prayer was carrying a demon. It would try and strangle him in the night. You may believe that demons exist, or not, but after we prayed he was OK as he gave his life to Jesus. I've had experience in the UK of seeing that kind of thing but we just don't talk about it much. Well God obviously wasn't going to ease me in gently! Thankfully no manifestations, just a small voice confirming that it was done in my ear and a testimony the next day saying the problems he had experienced in the night had stopped. Praise God! I hadn't even been here a day and God was already using me. The first fruits he called it. Salvation on my first day. Already the trip was worthwhile. The Lord continued being gracious and gave me words of knowledge and wisdom as we prayed with people. In fact I found out he speaks four languages which is impressive. I know also that he was finding out about me, very wise, I would have done the same thing.

When we finished we went off to have lunch in his mother's house around the corner. Lunch ended up being around 4pm. Meal times are different in Africa, with the evening meal frequently being just before bedtime. With the heat I wasn't feeling very hungry anyway. I also found out that I experienced side effects from the anti malaria drugs I was taking. They took away the desire to eat and sleep! Very rare to get those side effects I am told by my doctor.

I opt to use the toilet (you learn to make the most of those opportunities) and we had a meal. We say grace here over the food but it's more solemn, more significant. We have so much food in the UK that it's not always the case, so thanking God for a meal had more significance.

Turns out Mickey is one of eight children. I also met other people from America that day as they were gathering for a wedding. Mickey's brother was due to be married to a girl from the States the next day. We ate vegetables, rice, potatoes with gravy. Very nice, hot, filling with something called Ugali, which is a bit like a dry dumpling that you eat like bread and with your fingers, after dunking it in the sauce. You may like it, when offered it I will eat it, but not my first choice!

Sunday, 6th November 2011

The Sunday arrived and we spent time before the service at Mickey's mothers house and I asked him if he wanted to know what I was going to say and he said 'no' he was prepared to wait.

I thought that was brave. A stranger coming to speak at the church when it's the 12th anniversary service of the church that day, the reason why I had come all this way. he had never met me before. I looked at him during the conversation and was reminded of a panther! He told me his middle name means warrior! I felt nervous but tried not to show it, but the number of visits to the toilet might have given me away!

I went back to the field where the tent was moved for the service that day. Everyone made me feel welcome. I joined in the worship and dancing and watched proceedings and then it was my turn to speak. Mickey got up to introduce me and told everyone that dinner was nearly ready and we wouldn't be long. I heard this and decided to cut what I was planning to say, to be even shorter!

I learn later that I was in fact the special speaker for the morning and they had an expectation that I would speak for about an hour. They hid their surprise well when I had finished in about five minutes. I really didn't want to compete with lunch and God had actually only sent me out with one word. On reflection, it was a test for me - would I only deliver the word the Lord had sent me with, and would Mickey receive it with such a short delivery? I was going back to my seat after I had spoken and he called me back to pray in what I had said. He told me that everything I had said was confirmation for him.

We had lunch there in the field, under the tent with all the church members. The guests were given different food from everyone else.

This kind of thing surprises me, I like it when everyone eats the same. They would if they came here to my house. We would all sit down together and eat the same food at the same time, unless there were little people of course. It is an honour to be treated as a special guest and given such care and attention, but Jesus came for the least, to be a servant. I am happy to be treated the same as everyone else. Perhaps one day I will get to host them in return and I can do it my way. I am not saying one way is better than another, it's just good to explore culture and see how we do things differently.

Mickey hardly spoke about what happened. If he wasn't happy about my ultra short sermon he was very gracious about it and kept quiet. If the tables had been reversed I wonder if I would have felt the need to pass comment. We ended up having a service that day that lasted over seven hours!

As I am going to bed I reflect upon the day and how hot it was, with full sun, no clouds and at the end of the day, even being under the tent, I notice that I am burnt where I forgot to apply cream. When I was talking there was no shade and I had to wear my hat. Now looking back, knowing I have the record of the shortest sermon they had at that church that God was testing us both. I was tested to see if I would add to his word or just deliver what I had been given, and Mickey was tested to see if he would accept me with the one word.

In the afternoon we had eaten rice and beans, then church had continued with many pastors and other church leaders coming. They all stood up and had good things to say about Mickey one after another. Then he had asked me to say something and I didn't know what to add. I just wanted to pray. Before I came on the trip the Lord had spoken to me about only wearing blue and green whilst I was away. It was meant to symbolise my bringing a healing of the land. So I stood up and prayed for the land, claimed the land for the kingdom, all of Kenya, everything, and everyone in the country, that prosperity would come to the land. I was totally led by the Spirit, this was His mission and I was up for Him using me as he chose.

During the celebrations a white car had turned up and people got out, one dressed in a white suit – amazing! I was impressed with it. His name is Bernard and he sat next to me. I will always remember his message on passion.

It was exactly why I was there because of my passion to do all God wants of me. No holding back, no restrictions – it's all for the king of Glory.

We finished about 7pm, the whole day doing church. The whole day praying and worshipping the Lord, getting ready for heaven. We all piled into a car back to the flat, hot tea, food, prayers and bed, it had been a long day.

Monday I rested. We had toasties for breakfast with grated carrot and onion, really nice. I read the bible, talked, learned. In the evening a man arrived called George. Mickey and George sat talking in Swahili.

I asked the Holy Spirit to translate but it was private and He is such a gentleman he wouldn't. I was led to a scripture in Revelations 2 about hidden manna. I didn't know who it was for and went to praise God with my MP3 player. The spirit descended and I was filled with the Spirit of God and started to giggle. I went to giggle with Rozah a bit in the kitchen and eventually went back to the men and their meeting. They were standing up and Mickey was praying before George left. God immediately gave me a picture for George and before he left I spoke out, asked him to wait, I had half a picture but I couldn't get any more. So I asked George could I just do what God was showing me. He wasn't confident but said "yes". I started poking him in the chest, once, twice, three times, over and over and as I did the words started to come about being pushed to the edge, about him being tested.

Then when I had finished Mickey explained that Pastor George had just been evicted from his home. Many Pastors are, they learn what it's like for those they serve. So George was homeless and I knew I wasn't to do anything to help him practically, but I remembered the scripture about hidden manna and shared it with him. Sometimes the hardest thing is when the Holy Spirit wants you to wait and not help immediately but God had shown me this for a reason and I will carry what I saw then for a long time.

Tuesday

It was arranged on the Tuesday to meet up with Joseph, another friend I had met on Facebook. He picked us up in his car in Nairobi and started driving out of the city. We arrived at a hotel where he bought us lunch, the sort of menu you could find in any pub in the UK. I had chicken burger and chips. I thought that would be the end of our day but we were to be really blessed. Mickey and I were driven out even further to a tea plantation up in the hills. Miles and miles of tea plants growing. It's actually very good for the locals because it gives all year round employment. Tea can be picked every two weeks, 52 weeks a year. It was good to know it was a major exporter and adding to the economy. We watched a demonstration of how tea is processed, tasted some and left, educated and blessed. Joseph was on a mission to see how much he could bless us in one day. Next he took us to the escarpment overlooking the Masai Mara lands – beautiful views, amazing countryside. He brought me a Masai shawl there. We got back to the city in time to be jammed up with all the other traffic. It took hours to get back, but I had the opportunity to see some of the country.

I will never forget Joseph's kindness that day, taking us out, it was such a blessing.

I had trouble sleeping that night and found myself praying much. There was a burden to pray.

I was advised by one of the American ladies that if you go to a café with the pastors be prepared to pay for the order, it was good advice.

Many of the pastors I met struggle daily to live, there is always a need to pray for provision. These men and women who have been called by God have laid aside glowing prosperous careers. These are intelligent people with degrees, but they have submitted themselves to God's will and find themselves trusting God for even their bus fares. I didn't understand how or why that could happen. But I started asking questions. When the global economy slumped, food prices rose about 20 percent which means that the pastors were just getting by before, but now there is a problem. My heart is for pastors, I was getting to understand why I was here. I was hearing that God had a problem and he had chosen to send me so I could see it. Not just for me to write about it, but also offer any practical help I can. So I pay when we eat out. You never know the pastor you are feeding might not have eaten during that week.

That day we met at the Java café, just along from the Hilton and we always go downstairs where it is much quieter. That is when Mickey tells me he is having a meeting sat at another table and a journalist from a Christian paper is just about to come interview me! I was surprised to say the least. Monica arrives looking very glamorous, tall and slender with a big beaming white smile.

We talk for a while, I give her a word from the Lord and she is gone. I have been sent the article since that day and it also includes a word the Lord gave me later.

Before I go any further I must talk about the buses. They are what we in the UK would call a coach, with stairs leading up to the seats. Often there is loud music playing on the radio, sometimes someone sells things whilst we are there as a captive audience, and you can even get people preaching on the buses. One day coming back from the city a tyre blew under my seat and we just kept going! It was incredible. Anyway, it was on the way to the bus that morning that God had told me he had released 10,000 angels in Nairobi. 10,000 heavenly troops dropped in to the city. Curious, I wanted to understand why they were here, something must be about to shift.

Later that day, the Lord gives me a word for Kenya! I spoke to the Lord about that to release a word for the whole of Kenya, it was a big thing. I asked the Lord for confirmation. He said "Didn't I Ask you to wear blue and green as symbolic confirmation of what I want to do here?" I agreed "Yes Lord". "Didn't I get you to pray over the land, over Kenya, and claim for the kingdom of heaven?" "Yes" I confirmed. Then He went on to say "Didn't I release 10,000 angels onto the streets of Nairobi?" By this time I was smiling knowing that I had all the confirmation I needed of what God wanted to do in the city. I know that I had to share what I was given, that's what I was here to do, whatever God wanted. When I returned home I emailed the word to Monica, the reporter, and there it was in the publication.

I had the honour of sharing a few times at the Solid Rock International Church mid-week groups. Just small groups who come together and they asked me to share. The first one I talked about hearing from God. Something obviously I want to encourage people to do more if possible. There is something incredible about hearing from God for the first time. I still remember mine, so I gave stories and testimonies about how God speaks to me.

When the meeting was finished we shared bread and margarine and tea. Whilst that was happening I prayed for Alex, a young pastor sat next to me. I just put two fingers in the palm of his hand and prayed in tongues. It was as I was directed by the Spirit. I didn't say anything in English except 'Peace'. We stayed like that for a long time. God was using me to bring comfort to someone on the front line, that's why I was here. We had met on the fourth floor of a block of flats and it was pitch black when we left, with no lights on the stairs I needed help descending. Alex held my hand, I appreciated the kindness.

The second time I was asked to speak, the Lord instructed me to speak about living by faith. I asked for confirmation because I was talking to people who had done nothing else their whole lives. I thought that it would have been better if they were talking and I was listening. But at the end of it, Mickey was excited. He explained how great he thought it was that someone around the other side of the world would understand him, knew the challenges that he faced. I was surprised that I could make an impact with my testimonies.

After going out for the day I had started coughing, which was bothering people. A dry cough is one of the first signs of Malaria. I prayed and the Lord showed me that dust from that day out had got on my lungs. I knew I was getting sick. That night, Mickey prayed for me before bedtime and my lungs started to burn. The chest infection was healed but the stuff in my lungs went down to my stomach and I started to throw up. Not very glamorous. I tried not to wake anyone up but by 5.30 am Mickey was up asking me if I was okay. I wasn't really, I was extremely embarrassed. Spiritually I know I had to be strong, take care to pray things through so I wouldn't be sick. I had avoided sickness on mission before, it's an obvious tactic from the enemy. How could I have got sick! I was cross with myself that I had let my guard down, but God had put people around me to pray for me and care of me. The next day I rested a lot and ate little until evening.

On one of the days a group of us were taken to see the street kids living on the edge of some waste ground. They had put plastic sheeting up and were living under it. Young men and women too poor to live in the slums! Reading this again, writing it, even just saying it, always arrests my thinking. "Too poor to live in the slums". Two of the young women are pregnant and there are babies playing with the rubbish. I was shown how you can tell that they are malnourished, the kids had ginger hair.

Things were pretty tough when I was growing up and many reading this will have stories, but it wasn't like this. We talked, we prayed and they were fed. I walked away feeling inadequate. I wanted to fix things that's how I am. I see a problem and I want to fix it.

To walk away was difficult. To be Alex, the pastor called to love these people, to be their shepherd, must be a difficult job. Thankfully we are not to carry these burdens but to give them over in prayer to Jesus. Not always as easy to do as it sounds!

I had a long talk with Mickey that night about projects and provision. He told me some people come and they make promises but then sometimes just go and don't follow through. He had been stung by people offering to help, he had set things up to do good things, then they vanished and didn't want to know any more. I can understand if those whom you might want to help could seem a bit reluctant. I was ashamed of those who had come before, promising long term help and then, for whatever reason, moving on. I know things usually run in seasons but imagine you are paying for someone's rent and then you stop. The impact on that life…. Well, just imagine being forced to live on the streets yourself. The thing is, sometimes people change their giving on a whim. I made a promise to myself that if I were to get involved in a long-term project, I would have to be prepared to sacrifice things myself if I needed to. To ensure the help I had promised got through. Short term aid and support was all I was prepared to give at the time unless God showed me specifics.

I was invited to spend a day with the ladies as one was having her hair done. She was having false hair plaited in with her own hair. It took a long time. We were there most of the day. We ate rice and a stew with salad. We talked and shared and also had our nails done.

I can't imagine ever having that done to my hair. I spend as little time as possible working on mine.

As the week continues I am off back to the city to meet another pastor at the Java café, downstairs as before and the Lord has shown me that this pastor is struggling. It had been planned that I should have met him the day before but it never came together. Today was God's perfect timing. He arrived and I asked how he was and he said that he was fine, which shouldn't have surprised me because I wouldn't share that I was having problems with a complete stranger. We talked some more and then I asked again how he was and he said that he was fine again. So I came out and shared what the Lord had said. Then he shared that he was having a hard time, finding it difficult to pray. I wasn't surprised, pastors are always on the front line, always caring and looking after others.

We are all called to pray for our pastors, they need us to. The Lord had shown me what to do. I prayed that the Holy Spirit would fill him afresh, but God hadn't finished. I found myself praying that the joy of the Lord would come upon him, that he would laugh so much he would be rolling around on the floor of the café! I like those fun kinds of prayers. Well, we asked and God delivered. The joy of the Lord came down on us both and we started laughing. No rolling around on the floor but enough that at the end of it we both felt different.

I am telling you this story because God is good and he answers prayer, but also to say that is a lot of what I do, just praying and blessing pastors, much of it unseen.

It takes two buses to get to the church on Sunday and I listen to Mickey talk about " The Blessing", not blessings but THE BLESSING. It still lives with me even now and would be significant for my next visit, but then I had no idea of its importance. I also got to share and told testimony of how God can take the small thing that we have been working on for years and which doesn't seem to be doing much. God can take it and breathe on it and it can suddenly take off. One man plants and another man waters but only God can make it grow. It was a word for some of those sat there. But it also spoke to me again about the website I had been working on for so many years. I was again meeting up with pastors I had been talking with on Facebook. Another one had come to meet me. He only had sufficient funds to get him there. God had already directed me to bless him. Thankfully the Lord had told me before I'd left the flat that morning because the money belt I was wearing was under a dress! Not the thing, I don't think, to hitch up your dress in company to extract funds! (just a little tip for the ladies – plan ahead). I can't say I am in that place, prepared to leave to go somewhere and not know how I was going to get home. I thought I'd been brave enough thank you! We spent time over lunch talking about the goodness of God.

On one of the evenings when we were praying before bed, I started to pray the kind of prayers I pray when I am alone with the Lord. The hungry prayers, my prayers of longing and desperation, not for things but for Him.

The presence of God came into the room, it was tangible and wonderful and we all loved it.

I read that someone said that the people who just go after God are a waste of time, they never achieve anything because they don't ask for things they need to do the Lord's business, they just want Him. The scripture that talks about seeking his face and all else will come to you is the verse that comes to mind. I believe it is in the nature of the Lord to look for people who look for Him and be in relationship with Him, and out of that then to bless you because of His good pleasure. So if for the entire week I was to do nothing but spend time with the Lord and praise Him and honour Him, he would direct my steps to be a blessing and to be blessed.

It came to my last day and those I had met contacted me to say goodbye. I was already being asked when I would come back again. I was asked what I wanted to do on my last day. Mickey would have been happy to take me somewhere to buy gifts to take home, but I had come on a budget. I had come on the money the Lord had given me for the trip. I had enough left just to pay for the taxi to the airport and a little for a cup of tea at the airport. I explained that I only had a little left so ended up spending the day at the flat. It had been a fairly busy time but there had been much time just sat around. I asked if I would come back, my prayers that the Lord would bring me back. The plane for the UK was due to leave at 11.30pm and would fly all night and arrive back home sometime after 6am.

The taxi was ordered for 7pm, the traffic jams in Nairobi during rush hour are something to behold. All the shops and offices are in the centre and everyone commutes into town each day. I was told that people who had been there before me had missed their planes due to the bad traffic and even better is if during rush hour it rains as well.

With the taxi's in Kenya what happens the taxi is booked the night before, the driver tries to find your house so they know where it is when you need it. They have to come twice because none of the roads in the suburbs have names, none of the blocks of flats are named, none of the flats have numbers. So the taxi driver comes and you negotiate a price for the next day. Usually when you are on the way to your destination you go to the petrol station and the taxi driver will need your money to pay for the fuel! It's okay if you are in a hotel because there is sure to be a taxi camped outside but ask the price before you get in.

We leave at 7pm to be there in time. They ask to check my bag before I get to check in. I tell them they can but there is a lot of smelly washing in the case. Esther has been doing my washing for me whilst I have been in Kenya but it's all done by hand, a back breaking task. So I kept my washing needs to the minimum because I know that I can put it all in the washing machine when I get home.

You can buy washing machines in Kenya and I know that the houses they build have water storage under the house, so the likelihood of not being able to run it is minimum.

But with unemployment running high, giving someone work and paying them to do your washing would be a blessing to them.

Now I am all checked in and I wait in the Nairobi departure lounge. I purchase tea with the last of my money and am sat opposite a duty free shop and look at the chocolate. I realise I haven't really had chocolate since I arrived and I suddenly have an urge for some but I have no money. It turns out I couldn't even use my cards as the machines weren't working. I realise I will have to wait. I pray there will be someone nice to sit next to on the plane and read until my flight is called.

In the departure lounge I start talking to an American couple who are missionaries. We talk for a while and then I ask their seat numbers. You guessed right – they were right next to me on the flight home. Thank God for His answer to prayer. We were in our seats on the plane and the wife got out a bar of chocolate as I am telling her husband I was really fancying chocolate. The thing is, she couldn't hear me over the noise of the plane and she gave out the comment "I don't know why I'm getting this out". The husband tells her it's for me! God thinks of everything, it nearly renders me in tears. He cares about me enough to organise my favourite chocolate.

I spend time on the eight hour flight home to reflect on my time. In fact, I hardly sleep at all. That has become a bit of an issue for me this trip, not being able to sleep. I realise after I am back that insomnia is a side effect of the Malarone anti-malaria pills I am taking.

I think about the brief encounter I had with the Masai warrior I met getting on to the plane. He was wearing the traditional blue and red check clothing and about seven feet tall. I was telling him I was hoping he would be warm enough when we reach London. I also explained that someone had brought me a Masai shawl, his reply was fun. Now I have the clothing he said, I am Masai.

He was telling me that I had become a part of a warrior tribe. I am already a warrior of the Lion of the tribe of Judah! It felt like God was saying he had tested me with this trip and I had a right of passage to a new level. I knew I was different. My head and my heart was buzzing with all the things I had seen. My cry was for the pastors. What could I do to help them. All I met were constantly helping others. Not one I had met was not involved in social action, orphanages, widows, street children, and the list continues, the poor, those unemployed, the uneducated, the lost. I knew if I helped the pastors that would filter down to those they know need it most.

Psalm 76:9

When you, O God, rose up to judge, to save all the afflicted of the land.

I arrived home safely, just before Christmas and struggle to get into the season of excess. I am changed because I now have friends around the other side of the world whom I want to help.

I had seen so much, learnt so much and came away with a heart asking God why was it so difficult for the Pastors, why was it all so tough?
I came away with the desire to help but not to in any way get involved in a long term project because I was concerned that I wouldn't be able to fund it, and I didn't want the rug to be pulled on needy people.
Sat on the plane riding home, I thought that this might be the last time I ever visited Africa and wondered why God had taken me there and what He wanted me to do next.
So many questions.

Above the Poverty Line - Chapter two

It was hard to re-enter into the western lifestyle of the UK in the run up to Christmas after seeing the poverty of Kenya. I wanted to opt out and do something else, to pray and reflect, but I had to make the effort to get involved with the whole thing. It wasn't easy. I felt so different, and the season that had always held such excitement to me was now too much hype and not enough substance. Oh how God had changed me! I was the girl who would start making and planning presents pretty much as January came around. I would spend time thinking and planning how best I could bless my friends and family. I still want to do that now, but other things have become much more of a focus for me.

I thought things would all change when I came home but it was back to the same routine I had experienced before - long hours of prayer and bible study. After all the action, it took some adjusting. I kept asking God what I was meant to be doing and He told me I was already doing it, but I wanted more. I shared my experiences with my friends and put up a large banner for God to read which said 'what next?' It was a time of waiting again which can be difficult and frustrating. We have all had to do that at some point and it is about dying to ourselves and letting God do things in His timing.

The time of waiting is never just an idle time, but a time of inner growth if we enter God's rest and let Him change us ready for the next phase He is calling us into. The more we fight this time, the harder it is. Surrendering and yielding is not easy as it looks to the outside world that you are doing nothing, when in fact you are being transformed.

I was also talking to God about money. I would need to be able to resource things more, for home and the ministry. God didn't say much about that and I carried on my life with days merging, but He was speaking wonderfully through prayer and reading the word and I was growing in wisdom.

It wasn't until March 2012 that God started to speak to me about going back to Kenya in April. I was to go back to work with Mickey and to stay with them again. This time God wanted to really stretch my faith and have the tickets and the hotel booked the day before I was due to leave. I went into shock! I remember going around to a friend and crying that it was too hard. How could I go with so little planning?

I am smiling writing this, remembering the panic I felt. The Lord spoke and told me that everything would come in to pay for my trip before that date, but I wasn't to book anything until the day before I was due to go. This was all spoken to the girl who would plan a year at a time.

Could I do that? Did I have the strength to be so laid back about it all?

All the 'what if's' came to live in my head! The other question was about this training that I was going through, what could it possibly be for? To be ready to move at such short notice, what was that all about? I put my questions to the pending shelf in my head and focused on prayer and then came the fasting to go with the prayer. God had been thumbing through His diary and one day I would wake up and be told to start fasting. On checking my diary I would count 40 days until I was due to leave.

My fasting wasn't total, but seven hours a day from 7am until 2pm each day. Seven being the number of completion it seemed a good way forward. I would miss breakfast and lunch and then start eating after 2pm. Each day was like a mini fast of its own, leading up to the main event of my going out. I would be so passionate in my prayers about going, and then as the date got closer I would wobble a bit, and then perhaps a bit more, and then I would resign myself to going.

A few times the Lord has told me that He has to send me because there isn't anyone else to do what He wants me to do. He has asked others and they won't go. The harvest is ripe and the labourers are few, so off I go. I don't tell you that in a big headed way, it's just a fact.

It could be that you are the person reading this that had the call and convinced yourself it wasn't for you. I'm not really interested who it might have been, there is plenty that I need to focus on myself.

Mickey came to meet me as before and God had been speaking to him about me too, and I was there to work, and work is exactly what I would be doing. I had 7 speaking engagements in 12 days! Nothing was given in advance, God would tell me the night before what I would be speaking about the next day. I was mainly speaking to Pastors, which I love, and what I was there to do. I got topics from the Lord on poverty, dignity, sacrifice, death, vulnerability.

None of them were easy and as I would travel to a venue there would sometimes be tears as I made myself vulnerable so others could be blessed, knowing that God wanted me to talk about things that were, and are, painful for me to discuss. As I would talk the atmosphere in the room would change and then there would be an altar call for those who wanted to submit their life deeper to God and most would come forward. I was surprised by that and humbled at the same time. God was using me to make a difference and it blessed me and helped me to appreciate all the months of preparation.

Understanding being vulnerable was essential so that no one was stopped from coming forward and stepping into that greater relationship of knowing Christ. It was a worthy price and one that I will always pay to see passion renewed or a relationship with my Lord started.

Whilst we were waiting to be collected to be taken to the first conference the Lord started to speak to me about the Pastor who was sat waiting with us. I was to bless his feet! I knelt on the floor and placed my hands on his feet after asking permission and just prayed out a simple blessing for him and then got back up and we carried on talking. The really cool thing is that the Lord sent someone to the Pastor the next day and instructed them to buy him shoes. He had been praying for shoes and God delivered. I love it when He does that. I was even more delighted when the Lord repeated the blessing before I left by supplying the Pastor with a second pair of shoes. The double blessing right there in action. The Pastor concerned has his church in Kibera slums.

One place I went to was a lean-to church made of iron sheeting leaning up against another building. The floor was dirt and stones and there were some wooden benches. If it was completely full I would estimate about 50 people could fit in. They had a PA system which seemed to be turned up as loud as possible. I was asked to sit at the front on one of the few plastic chairs.

I did start to ask the Lord what I was doing there. Why had He arranged for me to come here?

He started to talk about the stable that Jesus was born in and how something so small and humble had been the birthplace of something that had changed the world. God likes to do that, take the least and make something great from it. I like that about Him, using the underdog in the world's eyes. If He can do that, imagine what He can do with us! I then saw in the spirit a large thunderbolt come and land in the middle of the church.

Fire was coming in a big way. The first day I talked about hearing from God quoting Psalm 19 verse 1-4. This talks about heaven always speaking. I love that. We can always be plugged into what God is talking about. The messages from heaven are not limited, it's just that we need to give it time. I prayed for everyone at the end of the session, praying for ears to be open and eyes too, to be more sensitive to heaven.

I was due to come back again the next day and the Lord was already speaking about what He wanted me to say but I had a mixture of Pastors and also the local children who had come to see the visitor. I had a message for the Pastors, a message that would be difficult for the children to understand and so I asked the organiser what he wanted me to do. He told me that they would keep the children away.

I knew that I had specifically come to that church for the Pastors so I could go ahead and share what the Lord had given me. There was one of the Pastors there that day and every time I looked at him I would get cross. I knew it was the Lord highlighting something to me. The Pastor was wearing a blue suit with a yellow shirt and the collar of the shirt was frayed.

It was the frayed shirt the Lord didn't like. I know why I was feeling that way because the Lord wanted me to buy him a new shirt. God really doesn't like His people looking shabby. So before I returned the next day I had to go shirt shopping, one pale blue large shirt on its way.

It was late when I got to the church the next day and I shared what the Lord had given me, I spent the whole time talking about being vulnerable and used the scripture from Matthew 27:27 which talks about Jesus being stripped in front of a whole company of soldiers just before they kill Him.

It was a scripture that the Lord would have me use again over the course of the visit. I felt that I should call anyone forward who wanted me to pray with them that God would take them deeper into new areas of vulnerability. I was expecting that perhaps one or two of this room full of mainly male Pastors would come forward. I was surprised when everyone ended up in front of me. Some came to kneel in the dirt, and I felt such compassion for them all.

It costs something to open up your heart and give Jesus the right to make you vulnerable. As I am writing this and remembering them all my heart goes out to God to bless them afresh and renew the fire within them, as I also pray for all Pastors out there, working in difficult circumstances with few resources and little encouragement. Bless them all.

That concluded that conference for me. The next event was to speak at another Pastors' conference where I spoke three times over three days. We travelled there by bus from the city and then a car up to the conference each day. The journey wasn't easy because it was the rainy season and what used to be road was now just a large muddy puddle.

I started to refer to Kenya as the mud lands. Travelling is so much harder to do because there are few proper roads with appropriate drainage. There was one point when we were trying to get back to the city when the road nearly got washed away. The real low point for me was using the drop toilet when it was raining really heavily outside and there was a hole in the iron sheet above my head, so when I squatted down freezing cold water would drop onto my back. It was at moments like these that I asked the Lord why I was here.

This conference was bigger and I was expected to speak for an hour at a time.

I used to find it difficult to speak for a specified time but now it's not a problem. I used to make notes and refer to them. Somewhere along the way the Lord asked me to speak without notes. I just write down the scriptures I want to use now, nothing else. As I am speaking the Lord tells me what to talk about. It makes it very easy. It's getting past the first part of standing there before a large group of people and having to trust God that He will pull out of me what He wants on any given event.

I never thought I would be able to do that, but it is actually very easy now. Amazing what God can do with us.

I had cried on the bus on the way to this conference because God wanted me to talk about death, about how it feels to lose someone and the feelings and emotions that we go through.

For the scripture God showed me the passage where Jesus goes up to the mountain to cry when he learns his cousin, John the Baptist, has been killed. I talked about how the Lord had taken me to that place in a vision and I had sat with Jesus whilst He had grieved.

Jesus so understands our pain and I shared that too. On the way back the Lord showed me that He wanted me to speak about poverty the next day.

Everyone, with no exception was living on far less than me and I felt so unqualified to speak to anyone in Kenya about poverty, but that was the subject matter and I had to be obedient.

The forty day fast that I had done before coming was to see the blessing released and on the last day of the conference that was what I was called to release. I prayed over, and anointed with oil everyone who wanted it.

I took a day out of the conference to visit Kibera because I knew I should go there. When I was leaving I was told that the British Embassy website recommends that those from the UK shouldn't visit Kibera as it isn't a safe place to go. It's reported to be the second largest slum in Africa, second only to one in South Africa. Two million people reside in Kibera. I can honestly say there was no one more surprised than me at what I found in Kibera. I expected people to be sat around begging, feeling sorry for themselves, drunk, on drugs and wallowing in a pit of self-despair. I couldn't have been more wrong. They were busy running stalls, selling goods, cooking, washing, and working.

There were even stalls on the railway lines that they just shifted when the train came and then replaced, selling food and essentials to those who had just got off after a long day working. I was impressed with the industry and how nice everyone was to me.

I felt honoured to have visited. There was only one incident that stuck in my mind. A small child was crying and I was told they were upset because they had dropped their money. Then I saw the child plunge its small hands into raw sewerage to try and find the coin! As I say, that image doesn't go away.

I think God was having a bit of a laugh sending me to a place where there weren't any even surfaces. Muddy, stoney and steep. I'm not good going down hills and needed all the help of Mickey and Pastor Steve who's church we were going to visit. There are many churches in Kibera, which may surprise you, it did me. Compared to what I had seen so far the church we went to was beautiful. It even had a floor that wasn't just dirt. We visited and prayed. It was mid week so there weren't many people around. We left via the railway line and caught a bus back to town.

I knew that I would go back, and I had a longing to speak at this church. I wanted to bring a message of hope. There are many organisations working in Kibera, you can see their signs up all around. People are trying to make a difference. I don't know how life changing the organisations are, and I pray that the money is spent on what people actually need, that nothing is wasted.

I thank God that they are there helping the widow and the orphan with medical help and feeding programmes.

I was also given the opportunity to speak at Solid Rock International which is Bishop Mickey's church in Nairobi. God called me to buy a bottle of oil and I will always remember what happened when I stood up to speak. God asked me to take the oil up with me. A small bottle of olive oil is expensive in Kenya. God asked me to pour half of the bottle on the ground even before I spoke anything. The whole atmosphere changed as soon as I did that. It's like everyone sucked in their breath and it went very quiet. God was making the ground holy, and I spoke about the double blessing and the triple blessing (Lev 25) and then prayed to release it over all who wanted it.

You might think with all that I would be ready to go home, but it wasn't time yet, I had one more trip to do and that required an internal flight to Mombasa. I didn't know what to expect except that it would be hot, and nobody had been holding back with that. It felt like I had stepped into a tumble dryer when I got off the plane, and within minutes Mickey looked warm too.

I was going to meet another Pastor I had been talking to on the internet and I would be speaking at his church. I had no idea what I was going to say other than to commission the church.

Pastor Ben's church had been running for four months and God had been speaking to me about claiming it as a sending out church.

We met Ben at the airport and He took me back to his home. We talked and ate and then it was decided a bit of a road trip was in order. We headed out to the beach and whilst on the road came across a flat bed truck with people in the back and red ribbon tied to it. Ben told me there was a coffin in the truck also and they were going to bury their dead. We arrived at Pirate beach, the public beach that the locals use. I was nearly the only European person on the beach. I took off my shoes and paddled in the sea transfixed with the people laughing as the waves came in. I was drawn to the joy. We walked away and I tried to ignore those who kept trying to sell me things.

Next we visited a place called Fort Jesus. Shaped like a person it has been there for a long time and we took the guided trip around. It was full of history. We then started the trip back to our hotel. We got stuck in a major traffic jam and were sat for hours. So I wrote notes about my talk the next day. God wanted me to speak out a word for Kenya. I found it interesting that He would want me to do that as there is a power struggle for Mombasa. It was significant that God would be highlighting that Mombasa was definitely a part of Kenya, so much so that He would speak from there.

God used every element of my road trip the day before to highlight what He was going to do.

I anointed the Pastor and his wife. I remember Ben, the Pastor, after the event saying that he had seen in a vision the exact same bottle of oil I had with me.

He knew that what was happening was from the Lord which greatly encouraged me too. The Lord also gave confirmation about this church being one to send people out. They have been meeting in a school classroom and on the outside of the building maps had been painted. I was so excited when I saw that. When we step out in faith God will always come alongside what He is doing and confirm it to us.

So, now the long journey home, fly back to Nairobi, pack and say goodbye, then the midnight flight back to London. I was already being prompted to pray for the next trip and I knew I would be back soon.

Above the Poverty Line - Chapter 3

One other thing came out of my April trip. Just before I left, God spoke to Mickey and he told me that he was going to be my Pastor. I left Kenya wondering about that. What was God doing giving me a Pastor in Kenya? Well it was God's plan and it works.

With modern technology it is easy to keep in touch and we are able to pray. I think in fact that I have more interaction with my Pastor in Kenya than many people do with the Pastor of their local church. God sent me all that way to meet a Pastor who understands how prophetic people work. How cool is that? I know there are people like that here in the UK, but that wasn't God's plan for me.

After prayer the Lord showed me I would be heading out again in July. God chose to provide the funds two days before I had planned to go. I was packed and had everything sorted except the funding, tickets and hotels. Nothing like living on the edge. I had been given a picture of a pearl, showing that all the funding would come from one place, and that is exactly what happened. I got a phone call two days before I was due to go with an offer of the whole amount. It sounds easy when I write it like this, but it isn't because it tests your trust in God to the limit. It stretches you to the edge and often I will feel like it is too hard and I can't go on. I went from praising and thanking God to feeling quite low and wanting to give up.

I get to the stage where I get numb and I just can't face or pray about it anymore and go off and watch a film and distract myself from something I have no control over. When you have prayed and stood for a long time, for me there is a limit. It may change over time, but this is how I cope with living on the edge. Sorry to disappoint if you were thinking I was super spiritual or something. I am human with doubts and the more God pushes me on the harder it can be. I am learning to just 'be' in the place of peace when the testing is going on, but I'm not there yet.

This is always a significant time when the prayers of others become essential. There is no way I could do what I do without the prayers of the saints. When I am at the end of myself feeling like it's too hard, God will send someone to lift me up. It humbles me completely when they offer to fast for me too. All that happened before the funds came in. Just a phone call and then I was really busy booking flights and hotels. It is also so important to share the good news with those who have prayed. I might be the one going but it took all our faith and all the prayers to make it happen. The fun bit is also ringing Mickey and letting him know I am definitely coming, there is usually a large 'praise God' from the other end of the line. I don't know what those around him think but knowing Kenya no one would think it out of place.

God raises up people who pray for me. When I am due to go out to Kenya the number of people who contact me from Kenya on Facebook increases and they all pray for me. God stirs them up to call me in.

I feel like an aeroplane and they are the guys on the ground with the paddles directing me in to land. I also get many contacting me to go to speak at their churches. It always strikes me as incredible that they would invite a near stranger to go and speak to their congregation. Perhaps God has spoken and it's clear for them that I am the right person to ask. But every time it happens I am honoured and surprised. I know that everyone who asks me doesn't just want me to go and encourage their church. I know that many want me to go and partner with them. I can understand that it is very frustrating to try and run a church with no funding, and so the Pastors look for those who will walk alongside them as partners. Seeing church members suffer and the church not be able to offer practical help through lack of resources must be utterly heart breaking. I can see where they are coming from. If every church in the developed world partnered with a church in the developing world to see them grow and develop, I wonder what the world church would look like?

Having no confirmation does make it difficult for those hosting me because they are asking me questions like 'where are you staying', and I answer them honestly, that I don't know. I wait until the money hits my bank and then look around for deals for flights and hotels. That's what happened this time, I didn't have confirmation until two days before. Thankfully God always has me pack my bag as soon as I return from the last trip so I am always ready to go at a moment's notice. I am still recovering from the jet lag and my head is thinking about packing!

I usually come back without much. Shoes, clothes, torches, toiletries, pain relief tablets, scarves all get given out before I come home, but then I am never short of things for long before God supplies me with replacements. It seems to be that whatever I give away gets multiplied back to me.

I remember giving away a pair of white sandals on one trip and got given three pairs on my return.

Back in June whilst sat outside waiting for church to start in the UK I was asking the Lord about tithing. Such a difficult subject to teach on because there is so much opposition to it. The last thing the enemy wants is for Christians to give their money to the church. If you haven't tithed before and wonder about its relevance do it just to upset the devil if nothing else. Most people are usually called to give their tithe (10%) of increase to their local church, but be open for God to get you to do something else with it if He wants you too. After all it's His money and He can do what He wants with it, can't He? Imagine if God called a few people to send their tithes to developing churches. It wouldn't have to be a great amount, but imagine the difference it could make to impact a whole community. Well I know that now I have written this that some of you reading it will already be thinking about doing that.

Some of you in shock and horror would tell me that the local church is short of funds to run their own programmes. I also know of many who are sitting on hundreds of thousands of pounds of money in the bank. That's just in case something might one day happen to the building.

Such a lack of faith hoarding what they don't need now. It's about trusting God for the resources when the need arises. Damming up the flow of funds from the church funds will actually stop the congregation giving. God supplies our needs, not our greeds!

I remember so clearly one Sunday evening when I was in church and I had my tithe all tucked in an envelope ready to put into the offering and I heard the Holy Spirit speak to me. He told me to give it to the guy next to me.

I was surprised and I reminded God that it was the tithe and it should go to the church. He asked me who the tithe was for and I said "It's yours God." Then He told me that if it was His, couldn't He do with it what He wanted? So I walked across to the guy and told him that God wanted him to have my tithe. The guy started to cry and I didn't ask any more. At the Tuesday prayer meeting the guy was there and he gave testimony about what had happened. He told us that he was about to give up on God, that God didn't seem to care for him and he was ready to walk away. When I passed over Gods money to him, he realised how much God really did care for him and he rededicated his life to the Lord. Awesome God.

I knew a few days after I arrived that there would be a celebration at Solid Rock International church for Bishop Mickey Okeyo on the anniversary of his becoming a Bishop. The church decided to include me in those celebrations. We were sitting in Steers, a chicken and chips café where we tend to hang out and they said that they intended to do something to honour me on that day.

I was overwhelmed and had to go to the ladies for a bit to gather myself back together. As it turned out all the gathered Pastors and Bishops came and prayed for me.

Before I left I was given a certificate of ordination as a Prophetess. I don't put it out on display but it's here somewhere. It was confirmation of what God had spoken to me on the 14th February 2011. That was the day that the Lord told me I had walked into the office of Prophet.

I know many struggle that people are still called to be Prophets now, but all the fivefold ministry needs to be working and active for the church to successfully finish all God wants done.

If I told people I was a Pastor or Evangelist they would have no problem, but Prophet gets a lot of bad press because it is so misused and many people are going around saying stuff is from God, and it isn't. If Prophecy is going to be used then we need a whole heap of discernment and a lot of grace and wisdom. Everything needs testing. I would be the first to remind people of that. I am happy for people to test what I am saying and if it is of God it will impact and change lives. If it isn't, then it should be allowed to fall to the floor and die. As I am writing this I am carrying a word around for someone, but it hasn't been the right time to deliver it yet. Timing is so important and I continue to ask God to make me sensitive to Him for His words and His timing and the love that He has for those I am passing things along to.

Thinking back to this visit, I remember God setting up a meeting with Lucas. We all went for coffee and tea and sat talking for a few hours about what God is doing and what He is going to do.

It was a great time and we were all encouraged. I have heard since that meeting that the word I gave from the Lord, Lucas took back, and out of that has so far planted five churches over three countries. I love to hear that what I do has an effect, but most of all I just get a lump in my throat knowing how amazing my God is and that He allows us to be used for His Kingdom and His glory. I was also delighted to be able to encourage those who support me and let them share in the knowledge of the fruit from one of my trips.

Originally when I was arranging this trip to Kenya I had planned to go to Tanzania as well. I even went ahead and got an entry visa. God changed my plans and I ended up going to Kisumu instead! God directed me to go see a Bishop Paul in Kisumu, it was a very last minute thing.

It was another poor area and an iron sheet church. God was setting a pattern of sending me to small rural churches that were struggling. The church was in the process of having their building taken away from them. There were plans to put a road through where the church building was. Everyone in the church was in low spirits, even the leadership. We ended up speaking to the church on a weekday. I shared with the church how God provides for me and how sometimes it is all last minute, obviously I talked for a lot longer than that, but that was the highlight. I was able to give specific details of the provision for the trip that I was currently on and how God had come through at the last minute. I was glad I went. We had been able to encourage those whom we met. God is faithful. I like what it says about faith in Romans 12:3, worth a read.

Over this trip I just seemed to be having lots of meetings with people, talking with Pastors.

It was a good trip I learned a lot, made contacts, spoke at churches. One that I went to was Kibera. I went back to talk to them about dignity. It was such an honour and something I will never forget. I was able to tell people who live in the slums that they get their worth from inside, from Jesus, and not from their circumstances or position. King Jesus has placed royalty in Kibera and we should never look down on those who live there.

Before I knew it I was back on a plane heading home, again not really knowing when I would be back, but knowing that something would happen and I would be flying out again. The eight hour flight is the perfect buffer to spend time reflecting on what had happened and getting my head back into UK mode.

What I mean by that is being in a country where it would be surprising to see someone reading their bible out in public or to hear someone preach on the bus, and the best for me is to hear worship practice groups singing out on the streets in Nairobi, just singing with no instruments and no microphone, just voices and harmonies, what a blessing.

So I come back from my time in Kenya and have to make
the adjustments to a completely different way of living.
Outwardly it's immediate, but my head and my heart take
longer. God has given me a heart for Kenya and the people
there and I find it hard to walk away.

But then there are the benefits of being back in the UK
with friends and family. You notice after a while that you
are changing. Things that were once really important to
you don't matter as much as they did. Take washing my
clothes - I've seen people in Africa wear the same clothes
for four days in a row and they don't smell or look
anything other than fresh. So I used to change my clothes
twice a day and put everything to be washed when I took
it off. Now I wear things for two days at a time. I feel like I
am doing my bit to use less water and I am still clean as I
still shower and wash my hair. (The two day rule does not
include underwear, just in case you wondered!)

When I am back I spend plenty of time listening to God
telling me what He wants me to be doing the next time I
go back. I also get the opportunity to carry on with writing
whilst I am in the UK. Every day I usually blog too. Every
day I go on Facebook and network - that's how it is. I am
building up relationships ready for when God wants to
press forward and I know the right people, in the right
places for when it's time. It perhaps doesn't sound
important.

Many times I have gone to Kenya and not seen a soul saved or seen a life turned around, but there are thousands of Pastors there fully qualified to do that. God wants me to do something bigger than that.

For that I need big faith and leading up to my next trip in September, that is exactly what He gave me.

For this trip the Lord asked me where I wanted to go and I told Him 'Kenya'. He eventually gave me dates and I waited and prayed as always for the funding to arrive. Knowing it can come in at the last minute I wasn't surprised to find myself packed and ready to go and no money for a ticket, or expenses. So the day before I just went into the living room and started worshipping God and gave everything to Him.

About 11am I heard the still small voice of the Holy Spirit telling me to check my email, which I did. A friend was wishing me a good trip and went on to say that if I had a financial emergency I was to contact them. I considered my position for a moment and knew it was an emergency so sent them a text. God had given me a verse from Ruth during the worship earlier and with good reason "Let her gather grain right among the sheaves without stopping her, and pull out some heads of barley from the bundles and drop them on purpose for her. Let her pick them up, and don't give her a hard time!" Ruth 2 15-16. My friend went on to offer me little bits of money they had lying around their house. I went and collected it and took it to the bank and paid it in. I was delighted that God had started to move and I had started to see the finances come in.

By 3.30pm that day nothing else had happened so I was thinking what could I do with what I had already been given to show God that I had activated my faith. I didn't have enough for my plane fare, but I did have enough to book the coach up to Heathrow airport, so I went ahead and booked the ticket.

Still nothing else happened, so by 8.30pm that night I went again to pray and I asked God what to do and He told me to 'go'. Go to the airport with my bags packed but no ticket - that would be an act of faith and exciting to see what He would do next.

I got up at 3.30am the next morning to get the coach to Heathrow airport and arrived there about seven am. I asked God what to do next and He showed me where to sit, which I did and I waited. I prayed and He showed me a vision of a man in a suit with a red tie. I can see it now, still in my memory as I am writing this. I knew that this was the man to look out for, he would be the one that God was sending to sort out my ticket so I could fly out that morning. Except he didn't come, the gate closed and the plane took off and I was still there! I asked God why it had all gone wrong and He told me that the man didn't have faith to come and help me. I wasn't angry, just sad. I was sat at the airport with nowhere to go. I was told to continue to wait and I wondered what God would do now.

I asked my friends to pray and had to ring Mickey in Kenya and tell him that I was at the airport but had been let down. It showed me that even if our faith is off the wall, others won't step up sometimes. It is easy to convince ourselves that we have got it wrong, that it was us.

Being sensitive to the Holy Spirit means doing crazy things and I am sure one day God will take me to the airport to buy someone's ticket for them. I had arrived at 7am and at 3pm I was still asking God what to do and was still being told to wait. I asked the Lord for another scripture and Ruth 3:18 was where I was directed which says "wait! The man won't rest until he has followed through on this. He will settle it today."

I took that to mean that God was sorting something out for me, so I continued to wait until about 6pm when I finally left in defeat. I cried on the bus going home feeling like I had failed.

You would think that when I woke the next morning my heart would be on the floor but it wasn't. I was full of praise and faith. The mood was so unexpected. I was asking God what to do now and He showed me that I had to visit a friend and tell them my testimony. I went and shared and as I spoke it out I was so moved by what I had been through only the day before that I cried. Around 3pm the day before God had been speaking to my friend saying I needed funds. They told the Lord how much they wanted to give me and the Lord had told them that it wasn't nearly enough! They were so obedient and I left with a cheque for my return flight to Kenya. I hopped on a bus to pay the cheque into my bank account praising God and asking that the Lord would richly bless my friend for their obedience to the Lord.

I met a woman in town after I left the bank, someone whom the Lord had me follow across town a few months before, but that is another story entirely, and I was telling her about the goodness of God.

She then went on to tell me about her need for a cooker. Her cooker had broken but she had seen a counter-top one that she wanted to buy but didn't have the money for. I thought about all the blessings I had so far received and told her to come with me and we went and bought the cooker. I got her to pray over the receipt for a multiplication of funds. If God were to multiply the money spent on the cooker tenfold that would be exactly what I needed for my expenses for my trip. So I was back out in town alone and asking God what I should do next.

I was instructed to go and buy myself a very nice lunch, so I did. Whilst eating my lunch I asked the Lord why was I there and He told me that I was celebrating as I would have everything I needed for my Kenya trip by the end of the day! God is amazing.

At the end of the meal the Lord showed me someone else I needed to visit. I arranged a visit and headed off to see them on my way home. I shared my testimony with them, I shared about the giving for the oven, I shared about our need of having an open hand like a runway. We have to keep an open hand so that funds can land and take off from our life. They asked me how much I needed for my trip and they offered the full amount I had prayed for earlier that day. A confirmation to me yet again that faith and obedience with expectation creates shifts in the heavens.

Two days later I headed out to Kenya knowing that my destination was Mombasa where I spent the week. I have to tell you that Mombasa is really hot, four showers a day hot. I have contact with a Pastor there called Ben and we spent the week with him talking and praying.

God was preparing the ground for something that He wanted to do. I love it that He also confirmed through Ben that I should be praying for somewhere for me to stay when I am there in Kenya. I need a base and that was the first thing Ben said to me one day when I walked into his living room. Confirmation is such an encouragement. Don't hold back if you think you have been given something to share with someone. It could be just what they are waiting for to take that step forward.

I got the opportunity to swim in the Indian Ocean on this trip. I don't usually take the time to see the sights but with the heat I thought a swim might be refreshing.

I have never been in sea water that warm. I was amazed at the temperature. It was like being in a bath tub. It was an experience I shall never forget. The sea was clear and the sky was blue and I just floated in the water letting God speak to me and enjoying the rest and peace. It was just what I needed at the time.

I came home and to the outside world nothing much had happened. It was probably one of the least productive times I've been in Kenya with regards to getting things done. I had only be allocated a week to stay there by the Lord, but to me it changed things in the heavens and gave me a time to firm up relationships. I get emails from people around the world all the time. Some, even in their opening message, ask for money. They are not interested in relationships and I know I am not the only one in the west who just switches off when bombarded with requests for funding. It's not that I don't care because I have seen the need. It's cutting out God from the exercise that I dislike the most.

If someone comes to me for money they are leaving God out from choosing who He wants to use to help. I want God's plans and the connections that He chooses. So I wait to be prompted by the Holy Spirit for whom I pray for and whom I give support to. If everyone did that and actually did the supporting I am sure He would have everyone covered, but unfortunately it doesn't work like that and many are left without the vital support they need.

So things were set in motion for my next trip which would be in November and December, just a few short weeks away.

I had prayed whilst out in Kenya that I wouldn't have a repeat of the Heathrow experience again the next time I was sent out. I can't say that I had enjoyed it much even though I had learnt heaps from it. I had learnt that even if I did step out I still had a way home, I was always safe, protected, and God knew exactly where I was. I didn't go hungry or thirsty and I was clean and had somewhere safe to wait whilst God spoke to me. It was a major step of faith at the time but as I look back I have experienced things since with much more danger and had the fullest of peace.

I prayed before I left Kenya that I would have my fare for my next trip as soon as I touched down. I prayed that it would be easy to pay for my flights. I wanted to speak at four conferences and needed to be able to say that I had my ticket and would be coming and God was faithful. As soon as I got back I was offered my flight money and also my internal flight money. I was so pleased to have that prayer answered and it made a way for me to plan what was coming next.

The next trip would be broken into four weeks with my speaking for three or four days then a day's rest and moving on to the next conference, outreach, pastor's conference, whatever it was going to be. I started in Kisumu, then a place just outside Nairobi, then Bungoma and finally had a week in Mombasa. I was blessed and welcomed and was honoured to be around when over 600 people came to faith.

I was fed and looked after.

However, there were two things about my trip I would have changed if it was possible. The first would be the time keeping. If you have a poster up that says your meeting is going to start at 11am and finish at 1pm, well, I don't know about you, but I would want to stick to that. I was called up to speak at one of those events and I was called to speak at 12.54pm and the Lord told me that I must finish at 1pm. I had six minutes to talk about the locusts eating away at our time and how it was important to not let things slip, then I was finished! The second thing that I would change would be how much expenses money the Lord sent me out with. He supplied enough for one week only and I was there for four.

I remember telling Him so well the night before I was due to fly out that I didn't have enough and I shouldn't really go, and He kept telling me to go. I went short of funds but lasted the time. God wanted to show that Africa could and would look after me by keeping my costs down. I wasn't able to bless those who I wanted to and I came back with an overdraft! When I came to the end of my funds God just kept telling me to keep walking!

I always thought if you were in the centre of God's will that you wouldn't get into debt for the Kingdom, but He does ask some from time to time to go into debt for Him. It's just another level of trust and obedience. When I returned home with an overdraft, it was less than two weeks before Christmas and the Lord told me that all my debts would be gone by Christmas. It's exactly what happened. Everything was cleared on Christmas Eve. God is faithful and He will do what He says He will do.

You are not going to be the exception with which He changes His mind.

It was the most amazing month with four events under my belt. I enjoyed the variety and the opportunity to share Jesus with so many. I wanted to help people go deeper and to have more passion.

If I can help one person get into conversation with God it feels good. After all, the Lord has been waiting since the beginning of time to have a conversation with you. Just think about that for a while. When He was planning the world and thinking about everything that was due to happen, He planned you, and I bet He had a smile on His face when He was doing it. You are so special to Him, so spectacular and He wants to talk to you and be friends. I'm not saying you should ever forget that He is God. I'm saying you were created to be a friend to God. Awesome isn't it.

On the last night, on the last event of a crusade, the Lord instructed me to stay in the hotel and not attend at all. I have to admit I was tired and welcomed staying behind. I could see the crusade from the dining room of the hotel and as it looked out over it all, I was praying. The last night of the crusade had the biggest harvest. The most people of the whole event gave their life to the Lord. I was delighted and not at all disappointed.

I had been aware of a growing understanding inside of me that crusades aren't really what I am called to. The Pastors and Bishops who are doing crusades are more than qualified to put an event like this on. They pray with passion and have many who have the gift of evangelism. I am happy to leave them to get on with it.

The thing I came away with from these events is the desire to teach Pastors, especially about Kingdom Finance. That was after all why I had to give notice on my job and to live by faith, so that I could help others walk on that path too.

Many Pastors in Kenya long to put on events but are limited by the funding. That is what I want to be helping with - teaching about the finance. Many in the church today don't see the tithes and offerings as a holy thing, just the church trying to take your money. Once you understand that God is interested in every single penny that you spend and what you do with it, then you start to get an understanding of the significance of your finances.

These revelations about finance came with the trip when I was able to bring ten micro business loans. I had already brought three over from previous trips and someone sent me with ten. I was able to pass them on to the church. It was interesting that they came at a time when I didn't have enough for my trip.

I knew it was a test - there will always be tests to see if we can be trusted with God's money. I came back owing money and that wouldn't have happened if I had used the micro business money! I know many are tempted with helping themselves to Kingdom money but I have been shown so many times that I own nothing and I am just a steward for the Kingdom and its finances.

I love it when God starts giving me my financial strategy at the start of a new season. I love how specific and directional He is.

If you are prepared to ask God about your money and mean it, He will show you down to the last little bit, and you know what, if you follow what He says down to the last penny you will see the most amazing miracles. When He tells you to give a dollar and within 10 days He blesses you with a 1,000 dollars because He tells you that you will need it -how cool is that?! Have you ever given a 1,000 dollar offering? I've been called to give a 1,000 pound offering, and it was really cool.

If you want to go to a new level with God blessing you, well perhaps you need to up the giving. Just saying...

So there I am telling people that living by faith is good and it works, but not being able to give much whilst I am there got me thinking.

In Africa it's all around the wrong way compared to the system in the bible. In the bible the idea is that a workman is worth his pay, and if you go to a church and minister there, you are working, right. So in the UK you would probably be given a love offering for your efforts to help feed you and pay for your travel and accommodation. In Africa if you are from the west they expect you to take an offering with you! Practically, if you are from the west the likelihood is that you will have far more finances available to you than the church you are visiting, but not always.

So the blessing they would have received from sowing into the visiting speaker's ministry doesn't happen. However small it would have been, it can't happen. God will not produce a harvest from nothing. Every time in the bible, if there was to be an increase, something always had to be given first. It's the principle on which increase is based and Jesus worked with it too - take the feeding of the 5,000.

I have encountered individuals and the odd church who understand about sowing and reaping, but it's rare. I know you are probably thinking I am hard expecting people to bless me when they have nothing. Well, I want people to be blessed and I know how the system works, so I won't apologise for speaking it out.

At the last conference, on the Sunday morning the Pastor told me that they were having a 'fund raising' that Sunday and I was invited as a guest. I have heard them talking in churches about fund raising.

That is what the world does, not the church. Fund raising is when people decide they want to get together and raise some money for a worldly project, it's not Kingdom. It's leaving God out of the event and you shouldn't expect a harvest from it. If you are in the church you can certainly ask for an offering for a specific project.

You may say that the wording doesn't matter, but God changes everything by the words He speaks, and so can we. If we don't call it an offering, then we are not giving it to God.

The next thing is that an offering should be led by the Spirit. It should be what God wants you to give. If God hasn't told you to give, you can still give from your heart, but if the person up the front is making you feel guilty or you feel uncomfortable about it, that's probably because it's not the occasion for you to give. I was at a service once, I won't say where, and the minister started asking for people to come up with their 100 pound offering and he would give them a prophetic word. Do you know what happened? I felt the Holy Spirit leave the room.

As quick as a flash He was gone and there was no anointing in the room. If God wants you to have something though, nobody can stop it from happening.

Anyway, back to the last conference where I was asked to lead the 'fundraiser' which I did. I told them how I had been called to give up things that were significant to me because God wants us to have nothing that can, in any way, be anything like as important to us as He is. Anything that you have that you say you couldn't give away becomes an idol. He will test you always on that one. So I got people to pray, sat in their seats and to just be open to let God tell them what He wanted as an offering. Then I asked them to bring it forward and put it in a bowl.

The first person hesitated when they arrived because it had been the custom to say how much you were giving which wasn't good. I asked them just to put it in the bowl and then it seemed like everyone in the place got up and brought something forward. Then God released an entrepreneurial spirit in the room and those who wanted it just had to come and shake my hand. God was working and I was blessed to have been there.

I always have mixed feelings when I leave Africa. I love the people and I know that I am doing something worthwhile there. People are friendly and welcoming and I get opportunities to encourage many people whilst I am there. Back home I am with friends and family but spend most days working alone. I know that won't be forever but it's hard at times.

Plus it was good to come away from Mombasa where I was having to have four showers a day to try and keep cool and left with over 30 mosquito bites which all itched!

I then have 8 hours on the plane to digest the things I have learnt, to process the things about culture and church in Kenya and to try and sleep on the overnight flight. God had me speak at some of the conferences about things I really didn't want to share. He had me give a session on the supernatural and angels. I was really surprised until afterwards when the Pastor told me he was just about to start teaching on angels!

God was faithful, I came home safe, well, with a knowledge that I had been used for the Kingdom. God had looked after me, but not in the way I had expected. Anyway I was back in the UK now, just before Christmas and it was difficult to settle back in.

I thought I had been through a difficult financial time, but God had other tests for me and I would need to cling to Him every step of the way.

So we come now into 2013 and the expectations of a New Year and a new season with God. What was He going to do with me this year? I had seen a lot of things and experienced much in the way of culture and methods. One of the culture ideas in Kenya is that if you are a Church leader and are visited by an international visitor then the leader will become your host.

They look after you whilst you are there in the country and help you connect to the people you want to reach out too. Now that I have been to Kenya a few times and have met many Pastors I sometimes get asked to give references for them. One day I met a Pastor in Nairobi from Canada and he was verbally brutal, asking about my covering and the details of how I operate. He was not gentle or gracious.

He then started to tell me how he had been ministering in the churches and I wanted to cringe. Why is it that people from the west are so keen for references about the way African Pastors apply themselves but it doesn't happen the other way around? I started to ask the Pastor about his covering because he needed to experience how it felt, and he seemed surprised that he too could be subject to these sorts of questions.

Personally I don't ask for references, I go where the Lord sends me and I have this gift of being able to see what someone is like inside without asking. I don't always get it right, but most of the time I have a pretty good idea.

The next time God called me to Kenya was in February 2013 and I didn't want to go! I mean I really didn't want to go.

Kenya was having an election on the 4th March and God wanted me to go and campaign with Mickey in a remote place in Kenya where Mickey was telling me there was no electricity and no mobile connection.

God was calling me to go for a month and support what Mickey was doing. I had instructions from the Lord that I must leave the UK no later than the 10th February. The finances came in at the last minute as usual and I left the UK with much trepidation. Mickey was already 'up country' as the locals call it and so I was met by Rozah, his wife.

I stayed with her for a day and then was put on a coach to Homa Bay, an eight hour bus trip. I had never been so far and so long on my own in Africa. I was constantly praying, but felt peaceful. We had to change coaches and I left everything unattended on the coach whilst I had to go find a toilet after 5 hours of travel! They have incredible bladder control in Africa. I don't know how they do it. I arrived safely and was met by Mickey at the other end. To say I was relieved would be an understatement! God had given me plans whilst I was there, for me to do some writing which kept me busy while Mickey went to campaign. Mickey had found me a place called Insipi that had a lounge and cafe in which I could hang out. I would take tea outside and sit under the trees, writing and listening to God. I was right in front of this fantastic view of Lake Victoria.

I could hear the lapping of the water and listen to the wind in the trees and the sounds of the birds and it was a haven for me.

Last time they had elections in Kenya 1,300 people were killed from riots and over 600,000 people were displaced. I found out whilst I was there that the UN had removed all their staff up until the elections.

But I know, as I expect you do too, that there is no place safer than in the perfect will of God.

When I arrived I went with Mickey to his campaign office. I wasn't booked in anywhere to stay that night. With the budget the Lord had sent me with I could comfortably stay in a hotel and eat out each day, no problem. The thing is, that if I did that I wouldn't be able to bless Mickey with funds to help with his campaign, which is why I had gone there in the first place. I had been given some work book keeping and I had been saving.

I knew I was being tested to see how much I was prepared to give. My time, my comfort, my money to see someone else succeed. Before long Ann came to see me at the campaign office and invited me to stay at her home. The house was full and they lived with no running water and no electricity which meant an outside room and a drop toilet. It would be the hardest challenge yet to be there for a month with five adults and five children. Two teachers and a social worker and they still struggle to pay for the children to go to school. Some days Ann's sister Elizabeth would get up at 4.30am to clean the house. You can't say they aren't hard working. I find it difficult to be constantly in the company of other people.

I am a reflector personality and I recharge by having time on my own to think about what I have learnt whilst with others. I also then have time to pray it all through and discuss it with God. This gives me His perspective on people and situations.

He softens my heart for which I thank Him. As it was God provided havens by the lake for me to do that, it meant that most mornings you would find me looking out at the islands with a cup of tea in my hand and a smile on my face.

My temporary office had the most fantastic view! They also had power down by the waterfront so that I could write. The only difficulty was the odd bird overhead, you know what I mean!

I would go out on some of the visits with Mickey and word started to get around that a white woman was campaigning. It gave our campaign a different edge. But the thing I really want to talk about is what God was doing in the background. The first time I joined the team to go out I was transported on the back of a motorbike, which was such good fun.

I started to talk to Edwin the driver and we got chatting about Christianity, after a short discussion Edwin made the decision to give his life to Jesus, and there whilst travelling we prayed the prayer of salvation. I was so excited. After we had the meeting I was back on the bike with Edwin and he started to tell me that he had asthma. So I layed my hands on his back, where his lungs are, and prayed whilst travelling a very simple prayer that he would be healed. I love it that we can be and do church anywhere. It doesn't have to be in a building on Sunday morning.

I love what it says in Acts 7:48 "However, the Most High does not live in houses made by men." He is out and about with me everywhere I go. Two weeks later I saw Edwin again as he came to pick me up one day and I asked how he was and he told me that he was fine and that the asthma was gone. What an amazing God we serve.

We were asked for a soda on many of the visits we made. Basically they are asking for something to have whilst sitting and listening to the candidate speak. It's not good practice and expensive.

I am told that once most MP's are elected they are never seen again so the people try their best to extract what they can whilst the campaigning is going on. Many then vote depending on how much soda they received from a candidate. I can understand both sides and I don't really like it, but it is for the country and the politicians to change the views of the people over time.

God had asked me to fast whilst I was on this trip, every day I would refrain from eating until after 2pm each day. I was leaving off the eating for seven hours a day and when I started to eat I would pray, believing for something incredible to happen.

The next surprise for me was when we went on the ferry to Mfangano. We went to stay there for a few days and we also went campaigning. We visited the local radio station and I got asked to record a message for the following Sunday. I had nothing prepared, but just prayed that God would give me something. I ended up speaking about salvation.

The manager listened to my recording before I left and he had a grin on his face. Being a Christian himself, he liked it.

We had a Muslim in our group who had four wives. As we were leaving the radio station I broached the subject of Jesus with him, and he told me that because of seeing God working through Mickey he would be giving his life to Jesus and I was to see evidence of his change of heart sooner than I expected.

Next visit was to a group over on the banks of Lake Victoria where there were boat builders. They gathered to listen and it was usual practice for someone to pray before we started. I was surprised and delighted to hear the Muslim whom I had only just been speaking to, now praying in the name of Jesus.

God was doing something amazing and He was letting me watch. I was so blessed. I was watching those men working on the boats with scruffy clothes and worn tools.

Most of them knew about God and were hard working, but there was a hard edge to them that day and the atmosphere wasn't one where faith was evident. Nothing much happened whilst we were there. We stayed in a guest house down by the lake, it was pitch black after dark. I do miss street lighting!

Thinking back to when we arrived, we met a guy called George who is a cousin of one of the guys who was campaigning with us. I sat with George whilst waiting for Mickey one day. It was very hot and I had gone off to find somewhere in the shade. I spent a little time talking to George and I prayed with him to come back to Jesus.

It was a very special day for me. I went to George's house before I left the Island. I spent time praying with him and his wife. I remember how delighted she was that George had been reading the bible since we had prayed when we arrived. It is always such an honour to be led to do that. I left with a burden for George who wanted to go to University.

It seems impossible with George only earning enough to feed his family for him to go to University. Well I thank God that His ways aren't our ways and I believe in my heart that he will get to go one day. It says in Romans 8:28 that God always works for the good of those who love Him.

Working around the islands I seemed to spend much of my time climbing in and out of boats, which must have been a real laugh for the locals because my balance isn't as good as theirs.

On a couple of the visits when I climbed onto the shore in a very unladylike fashion a group of ladies approached me singing in welcome. I got up and danced with them. It was a real honour. It isn't often that they get visited by someone of my colouring. When I thought of the remoteness of the islands and how their world is impossibly small, I would tell them I was from England and that I had stood on the Wembley football pitch. This they understood.

After a day visiting three fishing stations on one island we were surprised to hear what had happened after we left. Calls started to arrive the next day telling us about the size of the catches they received that night, not just from one of the fishing stations, but all three.

God had blessed us and they were aware that God had been there. Signs and wonders. It was lovely to hear about this. It's the sort of thing that you expect to hear about in your lifetime, but not something that is easy to get your head around when it happens. Bless those people, tucked away on remote islands, living life day to day, hand to mouth. I pray God continues to do mighty signs and wonders for His Kingdom and His Glory.

At the end of that day when we arrived back at the guest house I sat down to wait for the gates to be opened for us and found that I couldn't get up. It just wouldn't happen. My body was so tired, I had hit a wall and just wanted them to leave me right there with the fire flies and the lake and I didn't and couldn't move. So they helped me up and walked me back and layed me on the bed. I felt very silly as I am used to looking after myself.

I am going to tell you about a conversation I had with one of the guys because it's going to be relevant for the next story. I was asking about what happens if there isn't a toilet around, and they explained how you just find a quiet place and use leaves afterwards. So we talked about the different leaves and obviously you avoid the spikey ones. The banana ones are no good because they are too shiny, and some look OK but can bring on a rash.

A lot to learn, and I would have hardly any time before I had to put it into practice. We stopped on one of the islands and the toilet was full! So I had to go in the bushes. I'd left my bag with someone so had no tissue. My first time with the leaves and no bad after effects.

We went to a few funerals whilst campaigning and it is usual for someone to stand up and share their policies at the end of the service, before the food. I can't ever imagine that happening here in the UK. But a large group of people are gathered, respects have been paid and then there is an opportunity to look at community matters. It's actually a very good use of time for everyone concerned. Whilst I was there I sat at the back and got talking to a guy.

I asked if he was a Christian, which he wasn't and eventually he said that he would like to become one. I offered to pray and just sat on the chairs at the back of the service he gave his life to Jesus. It was so easy and just flowed. I thank God for allowing me the honour to see that happen, it will always be exciting.

I had been busy writing and we had been to so many meetings, but for me the most important ones were the community groups. I loved listening to what they had achieved and their hopes and dreams for the future. I would write down their aims and how little money it would take to get them to the next level.

I loved the fact that they had already worked hard and were saving, especially it would seem, for school fees. These meetings would give me such hope and would impact me so much that I now spend a lot of my time, and most of the support I receive on the projects I feel called to help. From church buildings, to classrooms, to feeding programmes, the list is endless.

Election Day was coming closer and we started to think about returning back to Nairobi. I had grown used to the rhythms of the days here, writing and talking politics.

I had learnt so much and felt that I had done very little to change things. There were a few occasions where God did use me and one of them was on a Sunday morning service.

We went to a local church in Mbita and the guy preaching made the comment during his talk about how all politicians were liars and not worth listening too and I was sat next to Mickey at the time! It made me really cross.

At the end of the service the church leader gave me the opportunity to introduce myself and I was able to share testimony of what we had seen during the campaigning. I started talking about how a man can be judged by the fruit that you see, and I started to share about Mickey's fruit during the time we were there. I told them that Mickey had led 12 people to faith in the high street, how we had seen people healed, and how we had also experienced signs and wonders. It makes me realise how often God uses something that isn't right to make us cross with a situation and that gives us passion to be bold, stand up, and say something. What are you passionate about?

At one of the other church meetings we went to the other candidate was also there, I loved the wisdom with which the Pastor handled it.

It was an interesting service. The man they had in to preach, whose name I cannot remember, was calling people up with prayer through words of knowledge, and words of wisdom I found myself walking to the front which surprised him because I had not responded to a call, He came over and shook my hand and I told him that I had come forward because he had a word for me. He considered it for a moment as I knew he would have to, as he was asking God what to do next.

He sent me back to my seat after telling me that I would be called up later. It is rare for me to be given a word by someone else, so I was interested to see what he would say. A little while later he called me up and spoke into my life words of confirmation about my being in Mbita, this being the start of something, and about the fact I would be working with widows. I don't remember anything else of significance. I was also asked there to get up and introduce myself and I just shared how God had sent me there to campaign with Mickey. Campaigning wasn't something I ever expected to be doing but God will use us to do the most unexpected things if we are open to seeing His Kingdom plans come to pass. How open are you to allowing God to use you for whatever He wants?

So Election Day was coming and I had so much peace. I knew that I would be safe. God had told me that I would be and I was standing on that. There was so much talk about what had happened the last time, so many killed and hundreds of thousands displaced. The churches had taken the call to pray for peace seriously and that makes so much difference. Isn't it incredible that just talking to God can change our environment, our hearts and our countries.

Many of the buses weren't working on the day after the elections and enterprising people had bumped up their prices for the ones that were. There was electricity in the air, like everyone was waiting to see if everyone else would start something. We had to take a different route to get back to Nairobi and the driver wasn't a happy man, but we got there by evening with no events.

I am thankful that we are always able to pray and ask God to protect us on our journeys.

Mickey and I arrived tired and hungry so we headed off to a cafe for some food. It wasn't long before Mickey headed off to catch up with some friends and I was left in the cafe with the luggage. God started to speak about what I was to be doing next. It was so clear and it was just like I was sat there having a conversation with Jesus. I love it when heaven downloads instructions in such a clear way.

I thank God that He never leaves us with a void, but always has the next step firmly established ready for us to walk into. I am a firm believer of just trusting God with the next thing when I can see something is over. I may have to go back to God and ask why something didn't happen, or stopped, but I am forward thinking because we don't live in the past.

Mickey and I prayed about what God had shown me before I left Kenya and when we had finished praying we both opened our eyes and the room was foggy. The cloud had come down and we were there in the glory. Such wonderful confirmation that heaven was with us.

So God had been talking about the way forward and I knew that I would be back soon.

Every time, God would send me back to Kenya. I have had invitations to many nations, but I kept going back to Kenya. In terms of how much people earn per day, Kenya and East Africa are shown to be some of the poorest areas in the world. There are rich people in Kenya with some incredible houses and even swimming pools. These are the people who have to pay for guards to look after what they have. The divide between the rich and the poor is like either living on earth, or the moon, the contrast is that extreme.

This trip I was off, back to Mfangano and it would be the most physically demanding trip so far. I wondered why the Lord had me going out on long walks before I went. He had told me that I would need to build up my stamina and He was right.

It's hours of travelling to get to the island and we divided it up into a few days. I would end up spending a week there and once you get there you realise that you also have to do all the travelling to get back! I was going to stay with Mickey's mother in her house on the Island. When you get there, in the compound there are other houses. All the sons are expected to build a house there as it's a rite of passage to adulthood. The girls get no claim to the land, or the rights to build there, which for someone like me from the west seems unfair, as I believe in equal rights and opportunities for both sexes.

The compound is on the edge of the island overlooking the lake, it's also quite high up and you can see for miles.

Life is going on all around and then you look up and are just arrested by the view. I find water so peaceful and during my free time I would put a chair under a tree and just sit sewing happily and full of peace looking out onto the lake. Not that there was much free time!

Mickey had my schedule full, starting with Sunday where I was asked to speak at Pastor Philip's church. We met in a small classroom and I spoke about healing and at the end the Lord gave words of knowledge for healing and we prayed for the sick. After that we went to have food at Philip's house. Well I say it is Philip's house but actually it belongs to his mother. Philip and his wife had a house but it was destroyed during the rainy season and so they are living with his mother.

I had taken a long time to walk to church in the morning. The ground was wet and so you had to jump from stone to stone. There are no pavements, no roads, no signs, no lighting. It's like being in the middle of nowhere, which is exactly what it was. I found the walking difficult and also the climbing over fences to get from one property to another. Walking through someone's garden was very strange, and even stranger was being directed into the house as we were passing to pray a blessing on their house. It took me hours to get to church, then another hour or so to go to lunch and now we had to walk back and it was getting dark. My energy levels were getting lower and lower and I started to cry because I didn't think I would make it.

I was getting slower and slower and I asked them just to go ahead and leave me behind. I just wanted to curl up and stop. They told me to rest, but I knew if I did I wouldn't get up again.

What with so much walking under such difficult conditions and preaching as well, it was too much. I finally got into the compound and my body stopped and I went down. I was finished. I had run my race that day and I had come to the end. They picked me up, marched me up the hill to the house and sat me down, removed my trainers and made me tea. I am, and always shall be, grateful for the care I am given when I am away. I slept well that night, you can imagine. The next morning I was feeling a little stiff.

Mickey had arranged for us to go to the local girl's boarding school on the Monday and they were expecting us. He advised me not to go because it would be too hard for me. I said we should pray as I don't like letting people down. So I prayed and God was there telling me to try, that's all, just try. So we prayed and headed out after breakfast. I was still painfully slow and Philip held my hand so I wouldn't slip and fall into the mud.

We got to the school and we were shown around. The conditions could be so much better. The kitchen was just a small hut in the gardens and seemed woefully inadequate. They wanted to know what I could do to help. I also got to speak to the girls about having a dream and a vision for their futures and God gave me some words for them. I was glad that I had gone.

We were meant to go back to Philip's house for lunch but we headed straight back to where we had come from. I couldn't risk not being able to make it back.

We made it and I was OK. They kept telling me how proud of me they were on the walking and what they had heard me say and it make me glad. I had tried and in my trying I had shown the girls that they can amount to something - that God does love them enough to send someone all that way just to tell them that they matter.

I have been questioned many times by those in the UK about why I spend money on airfares when I could just send the money. Africa has been having handouts for many years from the west and in some areas it has changed things a little and in some nothing seems to have changed at all. When I go to Kenya they tell me how important it is that I go and the significance it means to the people that someone came and bothered, that they were prepared to give up their time to come and talk. Imagine you had never really had anything other than your daily provisions. You couldn't get out of that by yourself unless you were incredibly strong. I saw during that trip that we could help make a difference but not with handouts, but with working with people, perhaps just a few at a time, to help them expand their thinking and get a little more.

It might just take them up one level to say having enough to eat, or the level where they can afford to send their children through school. To have their own business and help them learn to save a little to iron out the bumps of life would be an amazing step forward. Yes, I have a big vision to change the world, but in little ways for each person I meet. Just going and telling people that they can do something is a start.

I remember when our son was growing up I would tell him that he could be anything he wanted to be. He could go anywhere and become whatever he was prepared to work for and that I would be proud of him whatever it was. I believe this is the same for everyone, that we were all created to be different, that God made us all to have that in us.

I don't want to pay for a child's education, but I would be happy to work with the parents to help them expand a vision to start their own business, and in doing so they can do what parents are meant to do, be able to look after their own kids. It was interesting that the more places I visited and the more I thought about things I was able to cross off what I didn't want to do and see clearly how I wanted to go forward.

On the way to Mfangano we had travelled from Homa Bay to Mbita on a bus and the bus driver had crammed as many people in as possible. They even put a board across between the seats to create an extra seat, and they made the person pay the same amount. I counted up the seats and God started to give me a vision for a bus. God spoke clearly about a community bus, one that would give employment to some and some of the profits from the bus would be sewn back into the community, for the church and community projects. That night Mickey, Philip and I prayed about the bus and I was excited that we could, in the future see something like that come to pass.

As with many things the Lord gives us there isn't a set time frame, it depends on us and on how hard we are prepared to do what God gives us to do. If we take the slow route and are lazy with the things we have been called to do, it will take ages. If we are diligent it will happen quicker.

I got thinking about the bus and I realised the difficulties we could face and the skills we might be lacking to take on such a venture. But God had already thought about that and would start us small, with projects that could be a learning curve to get us ready to have a bus. It's exciting to see things stepping up and evolving with hard work and experience. Even with setbacks and problems, the thing is not to give up but keep going.

The next day we were up and out again off to another school. To get to this one was more like rock climbing. I did not, and can still not understand how I could be slipping all over the place on the rocks and the Pastor and Bishop would be planted firmly wearing just street shoes! They were so patient with me! This school was a primary and I loved talking to Head Teacher, Mark. He has a plan and a vision to expand and such a heart to see things improve.

I knew I could work with them because they were already doing stuff, they just needed a little help. Later that week I spent an hour talking with Mark about the school and I left him excited with a different way of thinking about the problems he is faced with. I can't take credit. All the ideas were flowing from the Lord and were an example of how He can use us to help others in business and education use their resources better.

I sang with the children here, a counting song, and I tried to stay as long as possible so I didn't have to climb the rock face to go back. We were right on the shore of the lake and Philip went to show me some land that he had already told me that he was giving to me. It was right there next to the sand and the lake. For me it couldn't have been more perfect and a perfect place to rest.

There was another Pastor there that day who had a boat and I gladly offered him funds to transport us some way back. We joked as we went about the fact that the Island is meant to have many monkeys, but I hadn't seen any. I also had a go at rowing and we didn't go around in circles!

When I got back to the compound I found that the pale blue cotton I had brought with me to do patchwork was the exact match to the mosquito nets which had got ripped. I set to sewing up the holes. It was something I could do and be a blessing.

I had told Mickey that I had never seen an animal killed for food before and it was something that perhaps I should view. We got a chicken and Mickey took me outside to watch. I didn't know what I would feel but I thought I would be OK.

He stood on the wings and cut the birds throat. It didn't take long, not much drama and there was dinner. It certainly makes you not want to waste when you see the sacrifice. So I thought the chicken should have a name and we duly toasted to Matilda with our tea over dinner that night.

After dinner Mickey and Philip went off to a meeting and I put my chair outside and God put on this amazing light show for me. Firstly there was lightening in the clouds and then cloud animal shapes started to drift by like an elephant and whale. By this time I had a fixed smile on my face and I laughed out loud as another shape drifted past for my delight. Then as the light faded the fireflies appeared and there were tears in my eyes at the sheer wonder of all that I had seen. I thanked God for my concert. I told Mickey about it when he returned. I don't know what he thought, but a quiet night in with God can be breath-taking.

The next day we went off to a local school and it was dire to say the least - one teacher of about 30 children in an iron sheet building. There were no cooking facilities and no toilet either. They would need lots of help because the teacher wasn't even being paid what she was owed. Some of the parents were there and they didn't even seem to have a spark to get something going. I would have to be very careful to start something there. For someone that school could be a full time project just on its own.

That was the end of my visits. I would be leaving in the early hours of the next morning to catch a boat at 3 am. However, they decided that we should leave at 1 am because I am so slow. That afternoon people started to arrive, the school head, Mark and other Pastors that Mickey looks after. They stayed for food and they would be walking with us to the boat in the morning. It would be an exercise in patience for them as we would stumble to the boat in the dark.

Before that happened we had church. I prayed over each of them and I shared about some of my experiences. It was a special night.

We got to the boat and got aboard climbing over the other people who were half asleep and wrapped up like bundles because it was so cold. We passed many fishermen on the way back to the mainland. We stopped at other islands to pick up and drop off people and property. Thankfully the water was calm. The seat was really uncomfortable and I was so thankful to get off. I can't ever see me opting for that way again. I would be happier to head for the ferry and do it in style, even if it does cost twice as much.

I headed home thinking about the children, about what I could do to help. In line with my thinking I wanted and still do want to invest in one off projects to impact lives. I just want to start something and let the locals have the pride in watching it grow. I want to use Pastors to impact their congregations so that they earn a decent living, which means the people can give their tithes and offerings and the Pastors are fed. Just a small project, she says, smiling to herself.

I had been given my next date to travel out to Kenya and it had been confirmed as the 31st August 2013. God kept telling me that I would go in August. I had just got back from Canada and America and here I was with a week's turnaround to wash my things and get over the jet lag and be ready to fly again. I love the adventure of that. So everything was ready and on the morning of the 30th August I had 21 pence in my bank account to pay for flights, hotels, and expenses. I was totally at peace that God would come through. It was incredible that by 11am on the 30th I had all I needed and was booking tickets on the internet ready for the next day. This would turn out to be the trip where the most unexpected things happened. I ended up spending a lot of time alone with God and He spoke to me specifically on the verses about binding and loosing. I was given specific keys about these verses and others were also being drawn to look at them more closely. I meditated on them for the time I was in Kenya and it equipped me for the times that are now, and the times that are coming.

I spoke in Mickey's church and it was different this time too. I would find myself walking up to people and praying for them in the service, imparting what God had sent me to Canada for. I appeared different, even to my own eyes.

On my Spiritual birthday back in 2010, for a present, God connected me to an African Pastor in a place called Macharcos in Kenya.

The Pastor there would have many dreams about me and I had been emailing him for months. He also kept inviting me to visit.

I had been due to go and see him in March 2011 but I laid it down before I was due to go and God took it back, it didn't happen and I lost touch with the Pastor. I always wondered what happened to him and on this trip I was given permission by the Lord to go find him and say hello. I just expected a meet and greet, that was all. I wanted to see the look on his face when I showed him one of the emails that he sent me.

Mickey and I caught a bus leaving the city and it took us about two hours to get to Marcharcos. One of our contacts had found the church for us and we knew where to go. We knew they had a meeting every lunch time and had aimed to be at the service. We walked in as the Pastor was ministering and sat near the back. Mickey was telling me that it was a deliverance church, a place where demons are cast out. Not the kind of church you expect to find in Bristol where I live. I was informed that the area had a high level of witchcraft. I was surprised when the Pastor stopped the service and came to meet us. He then asked us to follow him to a meeting room at the back of the church. First he greeted Mickey and asked him where he was from and then he turned his attention to me. I just handed over the email I had brought and he stood up and started to pace the room holding his head. It was wonderful to watch, we had a big hug. He told us that when we walked in the Holy Spirit had told him to stop the service and come meet us.

We stayed until the end of the service and he had me share with those there how we had met.

We booked into a hotel for the night and had dinner with the Pastor and his wife. It was interesting to hear how God had looked after him.

The next day we went back to Nairobi after it had been arranged that I would speak at his church on the Sunday. I asked God what He wanted me to say and was told that he wanted me to give an individual word to each person in the church and there were likely to be about 400 of them! I did return back on the Sunday and got to speak to about 70 of the people there before I ran out of time. I was blessed to be able to share about the goodness of God and about hearing from God.

On the way back, Esther, my interpreter for the day was concerned about the bus we were getting into. She wanted us to wait for the next one. There was something about it she didn't like. So I asked God if we would be alright and God said that we would. So we prayed for everything and asked for angels to keep us safe and such a feeling of peace came over me. It was the scariest bus ride I have ever had in Africa, well ever actually, but we got back without a scratch. God was true to His word.

I headed home, originally knowing that I was going for a month, which was cut down to two weeks. It was shortly after I returned home that I understood why I was back early. The Westgate Shopping Centre was attacked by terrorists just two days after I got home. God had protected me again by making sure I wasn't even in the country.

I had plenty of meetings and talked to a lot more people than I have shared with you, but enough to say I came back prepared to move things forward and follow the leading of the Holy Spirit and do what He was calling me to.

I arrived back on the 17th September 2013 and for the sake of this book that is where my journey ends. But I do have conclusions to offer you.

On the 1st November, by the leading of the Lord 'On a Mission' was started to help people move forward with community programmes and micro business loans. We did quite a few projects and then were called to close it in December 2016.

I am still visiting Kenya and have done many things. I have been challenged by God and had to change my thinking on some of the viewpoints I have expressed in this book, but that is what God does as we grow in Him. I continue to live by faith, though sometimes it's really hard and I wish I didn't, but I would have to say it's the most exciting way to live.

We are still on Facebook and even though the charity has closed it continues, you can see what we are doing now whilst you are reading this by looking up On A Mission, and Solid Rock Outreach Academy. I also have a website called sarahparsons.org.

Thank you for reading and lastly all the glory for this book goes to God because He has been good to us.

Notes

All Bible quotes used come from The New International Version of the Bible.

Printed in Great
Britain
by Amazon